Tales of Old Grafton

Tales of Old Grafton

James and Margaret Cawley

Photographs by the authors

South Brunswick and New York: A. S. Barnes and Company
London: Thomas Yoseloff Ltd

A. S. Barnes and Co., Inc.
Cranbury, New Jersey 08512

Thomas Yoseloff Ltd
108 New Bond Street
London W1Y OQX, England

Library of Congress Cataloging in Publication Data

Cawley, James S
    Tales of old Grafton.

    Bibliography: p.
    1. Grafton, Vt.—Social life and customs.
I. Cawley, Margaret, joint author. II. Title.
F59.G7C38   917.43'9   73-104
ISBN 0-498-01277-8

Other books by James and Margaret Cawley:

Exploring the Little Rivers of New Jersey
Along the Old York Road
Along the Delaware and Raritan Canal

By James Cawley:

Historic New Jersey in Pictures

PRINTED IN THE UNITED STATES OF AMERICA

*Dedicated to
the six story-tellers whose tales
were the inspiration for this book*

Contents

Preface 9

Acknowledgments 13

1 *The Authors Discover Grafton in 1953* 17

2 *Customs, Traditions, and Way of Life in Grafton, Typical of Those That Formerly Prevailed throughout Vermont* 39

3 *The Windham Foundation, a Vital Factor in the Preservation and Restoration of the Historic Buildings of the Village* 67

4 *The Recording of the "Tales" by the Men's Fellowship Club* 81

Bibliography 116

Index 117

Preface

Recorded history is, it seems to us, the sum total of the life experiences of a people and, from such experience local stories and traditions are born. It has often been said that every legend and tradition has its foundation in some fact, regardless of how incredible some of the tales may seem.

The subject of this book is Grafton, the village and the township, originally settled two miles west of its present location as Middletown (middle-of-the-town) where it began in 1780. It wasn't until forty years after the original settlement that it was moved to the present location to be near the growing industrial activity along the shores of the Saxton's River.

On a lovely May day recently, while driving around the hilly country in which the first settlement was begun, we tried to visualize the physical situation those early settlers faced as they began to wrest a living from the countryside. Their biggest handicap was the forest of huge trees, some of which were of a diameter of six feet or more, which had to be removed before any crop could be raised. While it was easy to see, in our mind's eyes, the huge stands of timber that covered the land, it was difficult to understand how those huge trees were cut down with an axe and man's energy. Nevertheless, the settlers did clear the land and make it ready for the first plantings.

The cutting and burning of the trees of the virgin forest resulted in huge quantities of wood ashes, from which their first money crop came—potash, which was in great demand in the textile mills of Europe. Potash was made through the simple process of boiling the wood ashes in huge kettles. No capital was required. The trees were the basic raw material; the labor was arduous but had to be performed anyway to let the sun onto the land. This was the first money crop of Middletown, as it was throughout the colonies. It is not known what the value of all the potash produced in Middletown was, but during the Revolution it did bring one hundred dollars a ton. It did provide money for the support of the family until agricultural crops could be harvested. Actual money was scarce in those days and most trading was on a barter basis.

Reviewing all those things in our minds during that May day of our exploration, during which time we wandered all over the area, reading the names on the stones in the old cemetery, and locating the former home sites, the site of the potash works, and other evidences of the first occupation, we had a thoroughly satisfactory day afield.

On the road leading down from the town road into Middletown and just above it there is, alongside the town road, a bronze tablet on a large boulder. It depicts, in the form of a town platt or map, a layout of the original settlement. We urge our readers who may sometime be in Grafton to follow in our footsteps on that day of exploration and actually enjoy the heightened sense of history such a visit will bring.

It is an interesting contrast today to see the beautiful summer homes that dot the hills surrounding the site of the first settlement, Middletown.

J.C.
M.C.

Acknowledgments

The authors wish to express their gratitude to the Bellows Falls-Springfield *Times-Reporter* for permission to reprint a feature on the Grafton village town meeting that appeared in the March 9, 1967, issue.

We also thank Little, Brown and Company, Boston, Mass., for permission to quote from Dorothy Canfield Fisher, *Vermont Tradition*. Copyright 1953.

Tales of Old Grafton

1

The Authors Discover Grafton in 1953

For several years prior to 1954, when James was scheduled to retire from the McGraw Hill Publishing Company, with which he had been associated for thirty-four years, we had been planning and discussing where and how we would live after retirement, and what we should do to occupy our time. We were in complete agreement on one point, that the usual inactive way of life of so many retirees would not in any degree be suitable for us. Having always lived very active lives, we were determined to continue that way.

What to do and where we would enjoy living during those later years was the problem we had to resolve before doing anything else. Having published as co-authors two successful books, *Historic New Jersey In Pictures* in 1939 and *Exploring The Little Rivers of New Jersey* in 1942, we felt that our post-retirement career should logically be a continuance of our writing. We had some ideas for several more books, many of which have since been published. And so it was decided.

Princeton, New Jersey, the community in which we had lived for so many years, had advantages that would have been helpful in our research for the titles we planned to produce—principally about historic and scenic New Jersey. Then, too, the Princeton University Press, which had published our two previous books, was located there. However, much as we wanted to continue living there, we decided that we would prefer living in some part of New England, at least for a while.

Those of our readers who are familiar with the seven New England states will agree that all of New England has great appeal. During the past half century we have camped and fished in Maine but, much as we love that state, we did not believe we would enjoy living there because of the long and severe winters.

New Hampshire, with its gorgeous White Mountains and infinite variety of lakes and ponds, held great appeal for us. Two of our daughters had attended Colby Junior College and the eldest served on its faculty for a dozen years. As a result we had many friends in the area. This was a temptation.

But after careful consideration and many discussions, we decided that, for us, Vermont would be the state in which we should try to locate. We felt that Vermont had not been invaded by industry to the extent the other states had and therefore was more natural and less hectic. After all, what we wanted to get away from was the modern industrial activity and noise we had been a part of all our lives.

So the question was settled. We would live in Vermont if a suitable home could be found, near to, but not in, a village.

So, the all-important question of "where" being settled, we were all set to go. We decided to spend the entire month of July, a year before retirement, exploring Vermont to find just the right place. Instead of the usual motel and restaurant way of traveling, we planned to do what comes naturally to us—tent camp in the many fine Vermont state parks during our search. We believed that by so doing we would find a place somewhere in the southernmost mountain area, where the summers would be comfortable with cool nights and the winters not too severe, as would not be the case if we located in the northern half of the state. We had enjoyed the recreational facilities of Vermont for many years, so we knew the country and the villages very well.

Before starting on our search for a home, we obtained a great deal of useful information from the Recreation and Development Commission at Montpelier, from the real estate folks, and from *Vermont Life* Magazine. Our problem was simplified to some extent in that we were not interested in the very large old farmhouses with their sometimes large acreage, which might or might not be run as an operating farm with a tenant farmer. Rather, we wanted a sound house with a few acres, and of course a view if possible— a place that would not entail too great an expense for upkeep. Now we were keenly counting the days until July when our vacation and search would begin.

Using our real estate directories, we began our search at Bennington, then looked at several places in Arlington, Dorset, Manchester, Londonderry, Weston, and Chester over the next several days. In every place the local realtors were, without exception, very helpful. However, while many of the places we looked over had many desirable features, most of them for various reasons held little appeal.

The weather favored us for the first week and each day at noon we stopped at a wayside picnic area and cooked a camp dinner and at night camped at one of the State Parks.

Typical of the mountain scenery visible from the log lean-tos that are located around the perimeter of the mountain in Coolidge State Park.

Occasionally we encountered a rainy day, and then of course we ate our meals in restaurants and spent the nights at a motel. We camped for two nights on the top of Coolidge Mountain in the Calvin Coolidge State Park, our favorite of all Vermont parks. The park accommodates tent campers, but the most enjoyable way to spend a night there is in one of the log lean-tos that are placed around the southern perimeter of the mountain. They offer the best views, and also the finest camping enjoyment, with their board floors, and a large fireplace in front of each for cooking and camp fires at night. Another particularly enjoyable night of camp-

The magnificent view from the top of Burke Mountain in the Darling State Forest.

ing was on top of Burke Mountain in the Darling State Forest, at an elevation of over three thousand feet. On July 10 we awoke in the morning to a temperature of near freezing. The flapjacks and bacon tasted especially fine.

We continued our search for two weeks and examined many little houses and badly run down large properties, the latter obviously much too large for just a couple to live in. We still could not find a suitable place and began to be somewhat discouraged and wonder whether our dream of an ideal little place in the country, surrounded by mountains, near, but not in, a village, was going to be realized. In fact, at that point we had about decided to go across the Connecticut River and continue our search in New Hampshire. But in view of the fact that we had promised to look up a friend in Grafton, we turned south at Chester and drove toward that village.

The road from Chester to Grafton is a delightfully wooded drive. For some reason we had never been on it before, but we recalled that on a winter ski trip many years ago we had been in Grafton but had entered the village by way of Bellows Falls. As we remembered it, we had not been at all impressed, for the snow was piled in drifts several feet high along the village streets and it was a dreary, overcast day.

On this journey we expected just a short visit with our friend, but we had a surprise coming. As we reached the top of the hill, before dipping down into the village, we saw a scene of sheer beauty. The road on the right was lined with sugar maples and on the left with great clumps of gleaming white birches. Straight ahead, at the bottom of the hill that towered over the village, was what we later learned was Bare Hill.

In fact, the entire scene before us was very much like

"*As we reached the top of the hill, before dipping down into the village we saw a scene of sheer beauty. . . . In fact, the entire scene before us was very much like some of the Currier and Ives prints of a country village.*"

some of the Currier and Ives prints of a country village. To complete our enchantment, when we stepped out of the car to look around, we saw an obviously old country house of a size more in line with what we had been looking for. It was close to the road, an important factor when considering the amount of snow to be shoveled, with a beautiful apple tree flanking the front entrance. The owners were on their lawn and, seeing our evident interest, invited us in and gave us a cool drink. They told us to wander around as much as we liked and take whatever pictures we wanted to. Up on the terrace and down over the meadows of some seven

"Longview," our Grafton home, in the spring, showing the apple orchard in full bloom on the terrace.

acres, we soon learned, there was a view down valley of over twenty miles. Mountains closed it in on both sides.

Later, when we drove down into the village, we were told that a Mr. Earl Wright was the local realtor, and so we called and asked him about property in or near Grafton. During the next few days he showed us many interesting places, not only in Grafton but for many miles around. For various reasons none suited us. They were all too large or required too much restoration.

Finally, while discussing other possible places with Mr. Wright, who, we were afraid, had about given up hope of

Part of the seven-acre meadow of "Longview," our former Grafton home.

An everlasting stone fencepost of a type rarely seen today, but which were a common sight not many years ago.

When the shad bush on our terrace bloomed, we knew that garden-planting time had arrived.

Fiddleheads beside the road above Grafton as they appeared on May 15th.

Two weeks later at the same spot, when the fiddleheads unrolled into ferns (brakes), as they will appear all summer.

finding us a place, we asked him if by any chance the little place on the hill was for sale. Much to our astonishment he told us it was. It seemed the owner wanted to sell out and move to Florida.

Following the usual discussion about price (and could it be shaded for cash?) among the owner, Mr. Wright, and ourselves, we came to an agreement, with both parties satisfied that the deal was fair. We agreed to take title in the fall, provided the title search was all right, and made the down payment before leaving. There were some improvements we wanted made; we thought it a good idea to get them done before the following summer, when we would move in.

Our search and somewhat discouraging experience until we discovered Grafton were over. Now, having completed our deal, it seemed in order to spend a few days in the village that was to become our future home.

The Wrights had told us about a forthcoming event to be held a year hence, during August. The pending affair had everybody busy preparing, and in a great state of anticipation. It was to be the celebration of the two-hundredth anniversary of the granting of the town charter in 1754. A huge parade with many floats was to be the main feature of the celebration.

Learning that one of the problems facing the committee in charge was how to finance a professional photographic coverage of the parade, we offered to do the photography, in color and black and white, and make available 8" x 10" enlargements of the black-and-white negatives at cost.

We had a whole week left of our vacation in which to get better acquainted with the village in which we were to live. Somewhere we had read, perhaps in some of the state's promotional literature, that Grafton was considered to be one of the five most beautiful villages in Vermont. So for a few days we wandered around photographing everything of interest and during those few days received a totally different impression of Grafton from what we had during that earlier winter visit. We agreed that it had a charm and a scenic beauty that well merited the fine rating given to it.

At the time we were looking for a house, the 150-year-old Grafton tavern could have been purchased very reasonably, but of course it would not have done as a private home. It was closed then, but has since been extensively modernized without spoiling its former charm and is now one of the most

The town hall of Grafton. In March each year the town meetings are held on the second floor.

popular New England taverns, open the year round. The Windham Foundation, about which more will be told in a later chapter, spent a large amount of money adding more baths, central heating, elevators, and other modern necessities.

Incidentally, the prices asked for properties at the time we were looking were considerably lower than those quoted today. In fact, as is the case all over the country, today's prices are double, or higher.

As we walked up and down the main street, enjoying the many fine places along the way, some of which were quite old and reminiscent of an earlier day in America—the Town Hall, built in 1800; the Barrett House, built in 1787; the

The Barrett Homestead on Main Street, opposite the town hall.

The brick Congregational Church at the head of Main Street.

The Grafton Baptist Church, with its tall white steeple, is typical of the New England churches.

During the severe winters the Saxton's River is locked tight in ice and snow, as shown here.

*In late March the icy grip is loosened as the water begins to flow
again, with larger areas visible.*

beautiful brick Congregational Church and the white clapboard Baptist Church nearby, each with typical New England
steeple towering above the buildings—we were reminded
of something that seemed to be missing. There were no
parking meters on the streets! There still aren't any twenty
years later as this is being written.

The most prominent physical feature of Grafton is the
Saxton's River that flows through the village. At one time
the river was the source of power for many industries that
lined its shores. At that time the population exceeded a
thousand persons. Today it is only a third of that number.

*The Grafton covered bridge as it crosses the South Branch of the
Saxton's River, on the road to the summit of Bare Hill. It is one of
the few that have survived the floods during the past century.*

Having thoroughly enjoyed our tour of the village, we walked over to the old covered bridge that crosses the river at the foot of Bare Hill. The bridge, like others of its type in Vermont, is one of the few that have not been washed away in the floods. They were known by the younger generation of yesteryear as "kissing bridges." It was the custom during the days of the horse and carriage when crossing over one of the bridges to stop and enjoy a kiss or two. Today there are several horse and carriages that may be seen on the streets of Grafton in parades and on other occasions. Perhaps if and when one of them crosses the Grafton covered bridge, the old custom of exacting a kiss is still followed.

2

*Customs, Traditions, and Way of Life in
Grafton, Typical of Those That Formerly
Prevailed throughout Vermont*

*Tradition hands down the practical facts with more precision
and fidelity than they can be transmitted by books.*
—Daniel Webster, 1857

For the year-round resident and, in fact, for visitors as well,
who sometimes make a special trip to Grafton for the occasion, the annual Town Meeting, always held in March, is
one of the highlights of the affairs in the village. In 1972
the Town Meeting was the 195th consecutive one held in
the community. The institution is unique. During the all-day
sessions the voters have full opportunities to express their
approval or the reverse on such matters as road mainte-
nance, school budgets, and the like, which are important to
the residents and property holders.

While we lived in Grafton we never missed a meeting,

and we always felt, while attending them, that we were participating in and helping to carry on one of the greatest examples of home rule in a centuries-old tradition.

In Grafton, as is true in other Vermont communities, the moderator is the man who plans, together with the selectmen, the agenda for the meetings. At times certain issues arouse considerable discussion and heat and, as a result, meetings are difficult to handle. Grafton is fortunate in that a former member of the Vermont Legislature, the Honorable Fred Prouty, has been for many years its meeting moderator.

Naturally, in a small village like Grafton, any attempt to get the floor during a meeting creates considerable confusion. However, the expertise of Mr. Prouty enables him to smoothly handle the business before the meetings, and seldom has anyone gone away angry, or at least stayed that way through the luncheon break.

For the benefit of those who have never attended a Vermont Town Meeting, the coverage of a recent Grafton meeting as reported by John Goodwin for the Bellows Falls-Springfield *Times-Reporter* should prove interesting. The importance of the Town Meeting to the local people may be judged from the fact that the paper devoted to the meeting a full page of text and photographs of the people who attended it. Here is Goodwin's description:

It was, most of those leaving the Grafton Town Meeting declared on their way out, a good meeting, but one taxpayer was heard to say, "I wish they would tell us more about where the money goes."

He must have been particularly interested in details, for the Grafton Town Report this year is of the type that was once common to all Vermont towns but which is becoming increasingly rare as the great Megalopolis moves closer to the Green Mountains. It is crammed with all sorts of information residents want

The Honorable Fred Prouty, who has for so long a time, served Grafton faithfully as Town Moderator and in many other capacities.

to know about. What is the tax rate? How was it figured? What's the budget? Why is it higher this year? Where is the money going? Why? What's this about transporting the children to school? Who's delinquent of their taxes? How much does the teacher get a year?

Grafton voters studied the report with great care this year and many of them had questions . . . detailed questions . . . that put the selectmen on the spot for a moment before they could come up with an answer. For the most part those questions were answered, but one woman, after a long discussion over certain items in the highway budget declared, "I'm more confused now than before I asked the question." "Well," declared Mr. Prouty, the moderator, in a let's-not-take-ourselves-too-seriously tone that marked the meeting, "It's too bad you asked it."

Gentle banter between the taxpayers and officials kept the meeting going at a lively pace and nobody seemed to mind that it lasted from ten in the morning until about three-thirty in the afternoon, with a break for lunch.

The taxpayers not only asked a lot of questions about town affairs, they also wanted to hear the answers.

When one selectman was having difficulty making himself heard in the back of the room, a taxpayer asked, "Isn't there another selectman who can speak up down there?" Prouty replied, "There should be two others. I don't know. Down in Bellows Falls they say they've got only one who can speak."

On the whole the voters were in an approving mood but the selectmen and the school board by no means breezed past the voters with their budgets.

A move was made to cut back the proposed school budget of $2.44 to $2.32, but this was defeated by a ballot vote. In Vermont democratic fashion the voters simply wrote on pieces of paper, $2.32 or $2.44, formed a line to the ballot box and dropped them in. The higher tax rate won, proving wrong the visitor who said, under his breath, "In the privacy of the voting booth I would cut my own taxes."

When it came time to nominate persons for the school board vacancy that came up this year, a man rose and nominated Mrs. Robert Hazeltine, "so that half the persons in this town will be represented." The same voter had mentioned earlier that there were some dissident groups in town that wanted representation but it turned out that the man making the motion wanted to see a woman's point of view represented.

A majority of the townspeople agreed and they voted Mrs.

Hazeltine into office on a 50–40 vote over the incumbent, Harold Crawford, by secret ballot.

At noon the taxpayers took a break and all walked over to the church chapel where a meal that must have been the best meal obtainable anywhere for six bits (seventy-five cents) was served by the ladies of the Grafton Grange.

The menu included baked beans, scalloped potatoes, brown bread and assorted pies. Plenty of coffee of course. The beans were baked by Mrs. Arthur Wright and everyone agreed (of those who partook of them), that they were delicious. "She makes the best baked beans in town," one knowledgeable Grafton housewife declared.

The luncheon was under the general chairmanship of Mrs. Walter Kenyon. The scalloped potatoes, which were prepared by Mrs. Norris Bragg, the town clerk and treasurer, were also voted the most delicious ever.

As is usually the case, because many of the farmers had to get away to take care of their chores, many who attended the morning session did not return for the short afternoon meeting. Tuesday, March seventh, the day of the meeting, was one of the stormiest days of the winter and, as the storm became worse many others left early in order to get home before being snowbound.

Adjournment was voted at three-thirty in the afternoon. It wasn't until just before adjournment that those present learned the result of the secret ballot on the question of whether baseball, band concerts and movies would be allowed on Sundays. The "yeas" won out on all three.

There is another custom that is regularly followed each year during the month of March by Grafton farmers and many people of the village who have a few sugar maple trees along the roadside. It is the custom of tapping the sugar maples for their sap and boiling it down into syrup or maple sugar products.

When the winter snows begin to melt and give way to the first March thaw, Grafton sugar makers walk through their groves of maples and, if conditions are right, begin the job of boring holes into which spouts are driven, on which the sap buckets are hung. In some larger operations and where

The Earl Wright sugar house, showing the collecting tanks on the trailer in the foreground. The sap is pumped from the tanks to the evaporator pan in the house.

the trees are on a side hill above the sugar house, an extensive network of plastic tubing feeds the sap down by gravity to the large collecting tanks, thus saving the considerable labor of collecting bucket after bucket and carrying them to the tank.

With the arrival of the first warm days of March, the sap begins to flow freely. Ideal conditions for record sap runs are warm sunny days followed by freezing temperatures at night. This swing in the temperature range moves the sap up from the roots of the trees into the trunk and eventually throughout the entire tree. A previously hot summer, followed by plenty of snow and low temperatures in the winter, makes for greater volume and better quality of the end product—maple syrup.

According to legend, sugaring off began centuries ago when an Indian hurled his tomahawk at a maple tree. Where the tomahawk made a deep gash in the tree, sap began to flow down into a cooking vessel that had been left under the tree. The Indian's squaw, believing the liquid in the cooking kettle was water, put some venison in to cook. Having been cooked in sweet maple sap that became syrup when it boiled, the flavor of the deer meat was like nothing ever tasted before. How the Indians later gathered sap in larger quantities and boiled it down into syrup has never been learned. In any event it is a nice yarn.

During the early days of our first March in Grafton our friends Earl and Doris Wright asked us to join them for a day of drilling, tapping, and gathering maple sap in their several groves of "sugar bush." We gladly accepted the invitation to actually participate in the fascinating spring event. Early the next morning, dressed in our warmest ski clothes, we drove down to the Wrights' home. They were waiting, and soon, with Doris joining us in our car while Earl drove his tractor, pulling the large sap-gathering tank, we started for the first grove.

Despite the fact that we Cawleys were both in good physical condition and accustomed to the deep snows of Vermont, we quickly learned that walking through the thigh-deep snow without skiis or snowshoes taxed our energies to the limit. We worked as a team, with Earl drilling the holes, Doris hammering in the spouts, and Margaret hanging the buckets, over each of which she fastened a little wedge-

The late Earl Wright and Mrs. Wright tapping sugar maples in one of their groves.

shaped canopy to keep the snow out of the buckets. James kept busy taking pictures and carrying the filled buckets down to the tank.

Before noon we began to realize how much back-breaking labor went into the gathering of the sap and the other, later, work of cutting wood for the fires under the evaporating tank. Even figured at the minimum wage, our labor would amount to a considerable sum. We asked Earl why maple syrup cost so much in the market place, but hastened to add, however, that having worked in the grove for only a day, we felt that whatever it sold for, if it was our labor that produced it, the price would be too low.

Earl told us it requires forty gallons of sap to make one gallon of maple syrup. On an average four to six healthy trees will produce forty gallons of sap.

Having spent a lifetime in sales and marketing, James asked why, in consideration of the labor, equipment, and materials required, Vermonters bothered to produce maple products at all. They knew that, even at the minimum hourly return for their efforts, the price of the syrup should be many times what it is today. Earl's reply, typical of Vermont folks was, "I take in about four hundred dollars a year from my operations and some of the farmers who operate on a much larger basis may make several times that amount. Whatever the income, we believe it to be 'found money,' as we make it during the time when there is little if anything else to do. It may not be sound marketing philosophy," continued Earl, "according to the view of organized labor, but to us it makes sense."

We had inspected Earl's sugar house earlier and had noted the great quantity of wood stored in the lean-to shed adjoining it. On the day of our first sap-gathering efforts, the first job, after we had brought the first large collecting tank full of sap to the sugar house, was to start the fire under the big evaporation pan. In the meantime Earl had parked his tank near the sugar house and started the pump that would feed the sap up to it. We soon had a roaring fire going and Earl remarked, "It will take quite a while for the fire to generate enough heat to start the sap boiling and then, after it begins to boil it will have to be watched carefully, perhaps all through the night, before it reaches the exact temperature when it must be quickly drained from the evaporator to avoid ruining it."

A Grafton woodshed with the fall and winter supply of cord wood. Some of the homes still use wood as the fuel for furnaces and kitchen ranges.

The sun had set and there was a noticeable drop in the temperature outside the sugar house. However, we were very comfortable close to the fire.

Soon the delicious odor of the boiling sap reminded us that our hard day's work in the groves had given us a big appetite and, since Earl had invited us to stay through the operation, we decided to go home for some supper and then come back to watch the operation while Earl and Doris went home for their evening meal.

Later that night, when the first batch of syrup was drawn

off, we were treated to a delicacy known as "sugar on snow." Scooping up a pan of fresh snow, we poured spirals of maple syrup on it which then turned the syrup into taffy. It was delicious.

During the evaporation process the boiling syrup flows continuously into one end of the pan and works its way through a long maze of baffles until it reaches the "draw-off" end of the pan. When the boiled sap is drawn off, the most delicious aroma anyone ever smelled pervades the air all around the area of the sugar house.

Late that night, when the last of the syrup had been drawn off and the fire had died down to a point that it was safe to leave, we all drove down to our house for coffee and doughnuts.

Describing our wonderful day in words doesn't really do it justice. Perhaps the photographs we took that day will more graphically portray the event.

We don't know whether or not it happened in Grafton, but it is said that during the spring sugaring off in March 1775, a settler returned to his sugar camp and found that a large black bear had trapped his head in a syrup kettle and could not get it off. The bear was quickly dispatched, and it made a good supply of meat and a fine rug for the settler's cabin floor.

Vermonters seldom hurry or waste any motions. Vermont humor, and it is of course true of Grafton, ambles along, takes its time, and never wastes a word. The following bits of folklore and humor are typical.

Visitors are sometimes of the opinion that village and country houses are not properly cared for and maintained on the outside. It is true that some of the natives still follow the old custom of "fix it up, make it do." However, the reason in most cases for the apparent neglect and run-down condition of some Grafton houses is the old practice of letting the outside of the house go without painting and repair because it has always been believed that such neglect would result in a lower assessment. Actually, the idea is no longer valid; the assessors long ago caught on to the practice and pay no attention to it, especially in view of the fact that the interior is usually meticulously kept up.

"Albert," asked the judge, "Where do you live?"

"Grafton," replied Albert.

"All your life?" asked the judge?

"Not yet," replied Albert.

A farmer on the Chester Road was asked by a passing motorist, "Doesn't this hill ever end? I have been driving up it for miles."

The farmer replied, "You ain't driving up a hill—you lost both your rear wheels."

"Had to shoot my dog," said Zeke.

"Was he mad?" asked Zeb.

"He wasn't so danged pleased," replied Zeke.

Frequently, whenever Mr. H of Grafton met an outlander he was heard to remark, "He ain't my kind of folks, but I guess he's as good as anybody else, long as he don't interfere with me."

A guest of the Tavern asked a local man, "I hear you have very short summers here. Is that true?"

The Grafton man replied, "Last year it came on Thursday."

Later, when the guest was relating what he had been told to another native, the latter asked, "Morning or afternoon?"

It has also been said in another way, that Grafton has two seasons, winter and the Fourth of July.

The following appeared recently in the Trenton (N.J.) *Evening Times:* "They still do things differently in Vermont: Believe it or not a member of the Vermont Legislature recently offered a bill for consideration to outlaw the killing of panthers. The last panther killed in the state and doubtless the last one existing there was shot in 1881."

Another bit of humor we like is the following:

A New York motorist driving up the Chester Road asked a passing native, "What is the name of the next town?"

"Don't know," replied the native.

The motorist then asked, "What was the name of the town we just passed through?"

Again the native replied, "Don't know."

"You don't know much, do you?" stated the motorist.

"Maybe so," replied the farmer, "but I ain't lost."

Whipping used to be known as the "Beech Seal." Disputes over land titles, particularly in the land grants around

Grafton, were sometimes more effectively settled by a beech switch than by the Colonial Governor's Seal.

It is refreshing, under today's conditions, to observe the people of the little village of Grafton still following their old customs and traditions. But the "Beech Seal" seems to have been forsaken.

"And what is the Vermont tradition?" asks Dorothy Canfield Fisher of Arlington, Vermont, in her fascinating book entitled *Vermont Tradition*.* She continues:

> To those of us who live here it is as familiar and life giving as air or water and as difficult to define in terms of human satisfaction. Can any words bring home to a reader in New Orleans or Singapore the tang of an upland October morning?; the taste of a drink from a cold mountain spring?
>
> Certainly it is nothing fixed. Vermonters are fiercely unregimented. They will disagree with each other and with the Road Commissioner hour after Town Meeting hour, about where to put a culvert. They disagree with one another more often than they seem to agree, although you can't predict exactly what they will do in any situation, you can always make a close guess as to the sort of thing they will do . . . more or less.

and later she writes:

> If a special Town Meeting should be called in haying time . . . perish the thought . . . involving what a Vermonter thinks of as human liberty, with a close decision in prospect, no Vermont farmer ever lived who would not stick his pitch fork into a cock of hay, drive to town and cast his vote against any measure which seemed to him to increase Society's pressure over the individual man or woman.†

---

* Boston: Little, Brown and Company, 1953, p. 6.
† *Ibid.*, p. 12.

This quotation from Mrs. Fisher's classic, while dealing with the people of the state of Vermont generally, may be applied equally well to the people of Grafton and their way of life. There such things have been the custom generation after generation for over two centuries.

It is one thing to read about it, quite another to understand how this can be true, when things are so different in other parts of our land. We ourselves enjoyed the privilege of living in Grafton and getting to know and respect the people in the village and township, and so we can understand why they prefer to follow their old way of life. Perhaps the reason is the same as the answer given an "outlander" who asked a native, "Why are there more cows in Vermont than people?" The native replied, "We like them better."

On the first of May each year we, together with almost everyone else in Grafton, including children, parents, and even grandparents, observed the opening of the trout season. All sorts of fishermen lined the shores of the Saxton's River, from the fellow from the city with his fancy tackle to the boys using an alder branch and a piece of store string for a line. It never seemed important that anyone caught trout. Just being there was the thing, according to tradition.

In the spring issue of *Vermont Life,* 1951, the following short article appeared, which not only described the beauty of Grafton but also seemed to sense the unique way of following old customs.

To experience Memorial Day in a small Vermont village is to establish a deep personal contact with American history.

Grafton is not unique among New England or American towns in holding beautiful Memorial Day services. It is perhaps unique in being a charming and unspoiled village that has never been obscured by outward signs of modern life. It has no movies, drug

The old, narrow, dirt road that was by-passed to straighten the Grafton-Chester highway. This lovely scene is recorded on canvas and film by hundreds of artists throughout the year.

On Memorial Day, following a prayer and during the blowing of taps, the children of Grafton drop a wreath into the Saxton's River from the town bridge in memory of sailors lost at sea.

stores, no neon lights, no business section, and except for the installation of electricity, plumbing and telephones it looks much as it did fifty or a hundred years ago.

There is nothing of the museum atmosphere in Grafton. Modern life goes busily on, but because evidence of the past is alive on every side, its Memorial Day service seems to embody the essence of all Memorial Days.

We would like here to add our own observation of Memorial Day in Grafton:

In the morning the Grafton band leads the village children from the school house to the Main Street bridge for the beginning of the observances. At the bridge, following a prayer, a gun salute, and the blowing of taps, two children drop a wreath into the river in honor of the U.S. sailors lost at sea. This is followed by the usual custom of decorating veterans' graves in the local cemetery.

In the quiet atmosphere of the little village of Grafton the observances seem to us more impressive than in the larger communities of the United States.

Those of our readers who may remember how excited they used to get on the eve of the Fourth of July will be thrilled, as we were, if ever they may be able to be present during Grafton's celebration of our great national holiday. There, as it used to be everywhere, boys carefully hoarded their supply of fire crackers and rockets, waiting for the great day.

Having been told that in the village they still celebrated that day, and the evening before, in the old-fashioned way, we found it difficult to sleep while we lay on our cot beds on our screened porch, on the eve of our first Fourth of July in Grafton. Promptly at midnight, we were awakened by the roar of cannon fire as the sound rolled up our meadow from the village below. Following the cannon fire, the bells of both churches began to ring and continued all through

"One of our most memorable experiences in Grafton occurred on the eve of Fourth of July while we lay asleep on our screened porch. At midnight we were awakened by the roar of cannon fire as the sound rolled over and up our meadow from the village, followed by the ringing of the church bells that continued until dawn."

the remainder of the night. As we were lulled to sleep by the bells, noises of giant fire crackers, their sound volume amplified through the age-old practice of firing them in pipes or culverts, continued to awaken us. It was an exciting night that revived many fond memories.

On Fourth of July morning boys of all ages began their own special celebration with their fire crackers. We drove down to the village and here and there we were delighted to see farm wagons, outhouses, and the like perched atop a barn or other structure, where they had been placed the night before. Since such activities seldom resulted in damage to property, we didn't think of it as vandalism. Rather, it might better be described as mischief, as it used to be in the old days.

There is an old-fashioned word, familiar to most country people but seldom heard today, the word *ornery,* generally considered to mean "hard to convince" or "sot in his way." It is frequently used in "he is an ornery cuss." A good example of it may be found in the following story from the pages of the *Bellows Falls Gazette* under the dateline of September 10, 1841.

> GRAFTON—We are sorry to learn that Grafton is not going to be represented in the Legislature. We learn that following nineteen ballots the citizens went home without a choice. Grafton is one of the strongest Whig towns in the country but the Whigs acted like spoiled children who spilled their milk and bread because they could not have a favorite spoon to eat it with. We hope they never again are guilty of a like indiscretion.
>
> They have had, at this year's election a strong pull. On another year let them pull together.

An excellent example of the common sense and thrift of the people of Grafton is the holding of church services in the brick Congregational Church in the summer and in the clapboard Baptist Church during the winter. Both congregations unite to worship in whichever church the services are being held.

When we inquired, during our first year in Grafton, about this peculiar custom, we were given what seemed to us a perfectly logical answer, to the effect that it was less expensive to heat the Baptist church during the winter.

A former custom, no longer observed, was the request for volunteers to chop the winter supply of wood needed for the church and chapel every year. It used to be a gala day in the fall when the men gathered in some woodlot to cut the wood. The ladies of the church furnished refreshments and a good time was had by all. The Baptist church is now heated by oil.

Church suppers and strawberry festivals are still regularly a part of life there. The ladies supply covered dishes for the events and the money realized helps meet church expenses.

The Grafton Cornet Band, believed to be the oldest in Vermont, continues to follow the tradition of playing Sunday evening concerts on the village green, as it has been doing since it was founded in 1867. As was originally the custom

The Reverend J. Sessler addressing the people of Grafton on the Village Green as part of the "Stand Up For America" day activities.

One of the floats, depicting the tossing of the British tea into Boston Harbor by patriots dressed as Indians. It was a feature of the "Stand Up For America" day parade in Grafton.

in small communities, the band formerly played on a covered bandstand in front of the tavern. However, the demands for wider roads to meet the increasing traffic made a move to the village green necessary. The first drum major of the band was Mr. Francis Phelps, and for many years membership was limited to the families of the early members. It has always been known as the Grafton Cornet Band because, during the early days, all the instruments except the drums were horns.

Originally the band comprised fewer than two dozen

members and over the years sons and grandsons of the first members have been a part of the organization. In 1967 the band celebrated its hundredth anniversary.

One of the high spots of the social life of Grafton during the summer months is the Sunday evening concerts that attract visitors from far and wide. A unique custom follows the playing of each number. In addition to the hand applause, the horns of dozens of cars surrounding the green are sounded in appreciation.

The Grafton Historical Association Museum, located in the former post office across from the library, is a must for visitors. On display there are many mementoes of the old band, including the uniform of the first drum major and hundreds of other artifacts the people of Grafton have lived with for more than a century. It is well worth a visit by anyone interested in Americana.

It has frequently been said that the uniqueness of Grafton in one respect is that when the "summer people" originally began coming to the village, many of them established a lifelong custom. The natives looked forward to the arrival of those people and got to know them well and, in fact, benefited to some extent in a financial way, because they represented a good market for vegetables and other products.

Over the years the native folks and the "outlanders" grew up together. That is to say, their children did, generation after generation. Many of the latter, upon their retirement, have made Grafton their year-round home.

As a result, in Grafton, as in other Vermont villages, a one-class society flourished through the earlier years of the century. Until comparatively recent years, with the advent of skiers and other winter devotees, there has never been any noticeable class distinction, as it is known in other places. Today, even though it is possible to drive through the State of Vermont on such modern interstate roads as I-91 and others like it, the dozen miles from Bellows Falls to Grafton, except for a modern blacktop road, remains much as it always has. That is part of the present-day charm of Grafton.

There is no public water supply in Grafton and everyone is dependent upon driven, or in some cases, dug wells for his water supply. Incidentally, the old custom of "witching" with a forked stick of peach or willow to locate water is still carried on in the area. There are still a few people who can do the "witching" or "divining." For some inexplicable reason, the practice actually locates hidden water. Except during the time of extreme drought there is never any shortage of water, but in dry periods the noise of the drilling rigs can be heard night and day throughout the village.

At our place on the hill, the driven well in the cellar, 250 feet deep, never failed us. We were told by an old-time native that ours was a well that had never gone dry in the memory of man.

The lack of a public water supply does have one drawback. That is to find enough water to fight fires, particularly the serious ones. After the limited supply carried in the tanks of the fire equipment is used up, auxiliary tanks sometimes have to be sent for. The problem was solved very sensibly by a series of fire ponds or pools in the river, the former filled by springs or run-off water. We were fortunate in having, not over 50 feet from our house, such a pond kept filled from a little stream. It gave us a sense of security we would not otherwise have had.

When the supply on the truck is exhausted a hose is placed in the pond or pool and the engine pumps it up. Thus, under pressure from the pumper equipment, plenty of water is at hand.

The fire pond, fifty feet from our house in Grafton, gave us a real sense of security against fire loss.

Until recent years visitors to Grafton used to be puzzled and usually inquired as to the reason for the ladders placed against private homes, reaching to the eaves, with another on the roof up to the chimney. They were used, before the use of oil as fuel, as a fast and effective way to fight the chimney fires that were frequently started in the thick soot coating caused by the wood-burning furnaces and stoves. Every winter, chimney fires were a frequent occurrence and they could be dangerous, spreading throughout the floors and walls.

As a rule the fire department is called out in such cases, but less frequently now because of the use of oil. When such fires used to occur, and they sometimes still do, a bucket of water taken up the ladders and poured down the chimney would help check the blaze.

The technique in fighting chimney fires in Grafton today is unusual and it would doubtless amuse the big city departments, who are supposed to have more expertise in such matters. However, the Grafton volunteer department men do all right, and their effectiveness is due in large part to the inventing and making up of a unique right-angle supplementary nozzle of pipe that is attached to the end of the hose. According to Edgar McWilliams, Jr., Grafton's fire chief, "it's more effective to insert the pipe nozzle in the chimney at arm's length and much pleasanter than getting a face full of burning soot and smoke."

If the fire is really hot, as it generally is, the water poured down the chimney spreads through the floors of the house, which creates a real problem in restoring the premises.

Two old customs that used to be observed in small towns many years ago are still followed in Grafton. In that little community where the income level of many of the natives is comparatively modest, each year in December a committee is appointed by the churches to solicit funds from the residents of the village and township for a Christmas party in the church, with a gift for every child under the tree. Baskets of fruit and gifts are also distributed to the shut-ins, young and old.

We well remember from the days of our childhood the annual custom at Thanksgiving for the more affluent families of each neighborhood to prepare large baskets of food, which were distributed to less fortunate families in the neighborhoods. Perhaps a return to such customs everywhere in the country would re-create some of the standards

In the Wright house, now converted to oil for fuel, is this old Glenwood wood-burning kitchen range of the type that graced most country kitchens a generation or two ago.

—especially more consideration for our fellow man—that have somehow disappeared during recent years.

Another custom that warms the hearts of older people who may visit Grafton is to find, in the large old-fashioned kitchens still in use, the old Glenwood ranges. It is true that many of them no longer burn wood but are fired by oil, which is less trouble and cleaner. The one shown in the photograph is in the home of Mrs. Earl Wright.

3

The Windham Foundation, a Vital Factor in the Preservation and Restoration of the Historic Buildings of the Village

Many of the charming little villages of Vermont have lost their one-time beauty and spruce appearance, either because of the indifference of the residents or in many cases because of the limited financial ability of the residents to maintain their properties. Grafton has been fortunate in the steady increase of new people who have bought some of the rundown properties and restored them for summer occupancy. In some instances, where a village is part of or near a popular skiing area, such winter activities have benefited local residents in many ways, and their increased income has enabled local property owners to maintain their places better.

Except for a relatively few overnight guests at the tavern, which is now operated on a year-round basis, or for skiers who may patronize the dining room, Grafton has not benefited from Vermont's winter recreational activities.

Until the late 1950s, many of the homes and other buildings along the Route 121 approach to the village increasingly showed neglect and untidiness. In fact, that was true in the village itself.

Because of a fortunate circumstance, that trend has been reversed. The unexpected good fortune of the village came about through the establishment of the Windham Foundation, made possible through a large bequest upon the death of Mrs. Rodney Fiske of New York City in 1959.

Mrs. Fiske, who had spent many summers in Grafton and who was very fond of "the little village in the hills," contributed generously to many worthy causes in the village while a resident. Her nephews, Mr. Mathew D. Hall of Cranford and Mr. Dean Mathey of Princeton, New Jersey, both long-time summer residents of Grafton, were named as trustees of the bequest left for the benefit of Grafton. The funds were to be used at the discretion of the trustees. They decided that the preservation and restoration of historic private homes and the replacement of other buildings would most nearly approximate what Mrs. Fiske had intended when the trust was created.

Many readily available projects were at hand, such as the purchase and restoration of private homes, providing for the former owners a lifetime tenancy. Other buildings, too, were purchased, such as the old blacksmith shop. This was authentically restored and equipped with the tools and other artifacts that shops of that type used in horseshoeing and in the production of iron objects that could be purchased during the last century only on a made-to-order basis in a smithy. That restoration has been completed and the shop is now open to the public as a museum and attracts many visitors. As one stands in the building today, with the

The restored blacksmith shop, now a museum open to the public.

pungent odor of the original forge still there, the lines of Longfellow's poem come readily to mind:

Under the spreading chestnut tree, the village smithy stands.
The smith a mighty man was he, with large and sinewy hands.

Those who may be old enough to remember how fascinating it used to be to watch the smith shoe a horse or heat and shrink an iron rim on a carriage wheel will find a visit to the Grafton blacksmith shop a rewarding one.

On the shore of the Saxton's River, below the Main Street bridge, formerly stood an old building, the foundations of which were slowly being washed away and weakened by flood waters, until it was about ready to fall into the river. That too was purchased and restored, and today it is an attractive building in which an antique shop called The Village Pump is operated.

The beautiful restoration of a former house that now houses the Village Pump, an antique shop.

A very handsome building of colonial architecture was built by the Foundation to replace the eyesore that had for many years been the only car repair and service shop in the village.

Across the street from the new garage the old and decrepit garage was torn down and a new private garage

The village pump on the shore of the Saxton's River beside the antique shop, both of which are restorations by the Windham Foundation.

The new village garage is one of the most beautiful of the Foundation buildings.

was built on the site, next to the historic Clarke House.

Having made such an excellent beginning, the trustees of the Foundation were determined to continue the work, already evident to the people of the village and visitors alike, until Grafton could again justify its former designation by *Vermont Life* as "one of the five most beautiful villages in Vermont."

At one time there had been four stores on Main Street, but all but one had closed. Then the one remaining finally closed, because of the illness and death of the owner. The Foundation purchased the building and restored it as it had

The private garage for the Clarke House, built on the site of the former village garage.

appeared during the last century, and it is again operated as a store, with one side of the building stocking grocery staples, while the other is a gift and antique shop. The re-opening of the grocery has been of great benefit to many of the local residents who do not have cars to do their shopping in Chester and Bellows Falls markets, seven and twelve miles respectively from Grafton.

Not only was the former cheese factory, which stood until a few years ago near the present tennis courts, a market for the milk from local farmers, it also provided some jobs. The Foundation completed, a few years ago, a new cheese

The Village Store on Main Street is an antique shop and also stocks a limited supply of grocery staples and soft drinks.

The bronze plaque on the Old Town Road, showing the locations of the buildings at Old Middletown. For the guidance of visitors, small stone monuments with corresponding numerals may be found at each building site.

The Dr. John Butterfield home on Main Street, one of the elegant private homes of the last century, which now houses the village public library.

The "Doll House" on the Chester Road, Grafton, was built in 1823. It is now the home of Miss Dorothy Lausser.

The small village school that still serves as the grade school for the local children. Those children who continue beyond this school are bussed to the Bellows Falls High School.

The Grafton Historical Society museum, which houses an unusually large and varied collection of records and artifacts for so small a community.

An old-time country inn sign greets the guests as they arrive at the tavern.

factory, housed in a very striking building of colonial architecture, with up-to-date stainless-steel tanks and other machinery. Old-time Vermont Cheddar cheese is again being made there, and it is sold at the retail store, over the counter and by mail.

The most prominent landmark of Grafton has always been the old inn, or tavern as it is known today. It was built in 1801 at the intersection of Main Street and the Townshend Road. During its early years, travelers over the old stage road from Grafton to Chester by way of Houghtonville, which passed its doors, were here accommodated.

The tavern was run for many years by two brothers, Francis and Harlan Phelps. The survivor of the Phelps brothers continued the hostelry until 1953, when he decided that to operate it as just a summer inn was not profitable enough. Over the years the Phelps Brothers had made extensive changes in the building. The roof was raised at one time to permit the addition of an additional story with porches and balcony, as they appear today. Not having a central heating system, the inn could be open only during the summer. During the days of travel by horse and carriage, the inn attracted vacationists from far and wide.

When the building was offered for sale, Mr. and Mrs.

The Grafton Tavern as it now appears after extensive modernization of the interior by the Foundation.

John Wriston, from upstate Vermont, bought it. They installed a modern kitchen and concentrated on the business of attracting guests who might be induced to patronize the tavern's excellent meals, which Mr. Wriston vowed he would provide. Through extensive promotion (and possibly the prominence of Mrs. Wriston, who was a well-known author of children's books), the tavern again did an excellent business. However, it became apparent that, in spite of the increased patronage by overnight guests, which eventually made it necessary to accommodate the overflow in the private homes across the street called the Annex, a stable and profit-

The old barn is now a comfortable lounge for guests of the tavern and is used as a village meeting place. The loggia that was added connects the lounge with the tavern.

able business could not be established unless the tavern could be operated all the year around. Central heating, more baths, and other essentials, including an elevator, would have to be installed. The cost of such improvements was beyond the means of the Wristons and so they sold the tavern and grounds to the Windham Foundation. It seemed an ideal opportunity for the Foundation, and they soon began the extensive and expensive task of renovation. They completed the job without materially changing the old-time appearance of the building. The old barn, the sills, and some of the timbers that had to be replaced were beautifully restored. In order to preserve the weathered siding, all of it was carefully removed to replace the sills. All was then restored so skillfully that today it is hard to believe that it had ever been touched. The interior of the barn was left largely as it was, except for new floors and the addition of a huge fieldstone fireplace at one end of the building.

Connected to the tavern with the barn, as is shown in the photograph, is a loggia of old barn siding. Today the old barn is a popular lounge for patrons of the tavern and a meeting place for village clubs and organizations.

With the renovation of the tavern, it is again the attractive "centerpiece" of the village, and it is fast becoming one of the most popular taverns in all New England and far beyond.

During the fall months of brilliant color of foliage, with the crisp air and the tang of wood smoke from the fireplaces of the tavern and the village filling the air, a stay at the tavern is a delightful experience.

Other purchases and restorations are on the agenda of the Windham Foundation. Without a doubt, when completed it will have prevented what has been the case with so many others in Vermont—the slow disintegration of this lovely village.

4

The Recording of the "Tales" by the Men's Fellowship Club

The authors, while year-round residents of Grafton from 1954 to 1958, were active members of the Grafton Congregational Church. During one of those years James Cawley was Chairman of the Men's Fellowship group of the church. The club met once each month in the church chapel, and each year a program of interesting speakers on a varied range of subjects of interest to the members was scheduled. During the summer months when the native population was considerably increased by the summer people, securing speakers for the meetings was not too difficult. But in the snowbound winter months, it was more difficult to draw them from other larger communities. Understandably, they were reluctant to accept a speaking engagement in Grafton for fear that they might become snowbound and unable to get back home. Therefore most of the speakers during the winter months were local people with a narrower range of subjects. In view of that, the program prepared by Chairman Cawley for the winter of 1955 was quite a departure from the usual ones. For the February meeting of that year a story-telling night was planned, with a roster of local residents all of whom were long-time residents of the village.

Six men—the Honorable Samuel B. Pettingill, former Congressman, who agreed to act as chairman for the evening, and Curtis Tuttle, the Honorable Arthur Wright, Frank Wilbur, John Grant, and the Honorable Fred Prouty —were asked to serve as the story-tellers. They agreed to come to the meeting prepared to tell of events and experiences from their own lifetimes, those from the lifetimes of their fathers and, if possible, stories from the days of their grandparents. In announcing the forthcoming meeting, Program Chairman Cawley stated that the purpose of the meeting was, first, to provide an interesting evening for members of the club, and second, to record the stories on tape and later to transcribe them and have them bound into a book to be presented to the local library by the Men's Fellowship Club.

As a result of those previously announced plans, everyone came to the story-telling meeting determined to do himself proud and to have his contributions memorialized for the benefit of future generations.

On the meeting night, a clear, cold, below-zero February evening, with the stars sparkling overhead and the snow crackling under our ski boots as we walked up Main Street to the Church Chapel where the meeting was to be held, we were glad to get out of the cold into the warmth of the Chapel. When we entered, every chair was occupied and everyone was keenly alive to the novelty of the occasion.

In deference to the possible nervousness of some of the less-experienced speakers, instead of having them stand

The wood-burning pot-bellied stove that heated the chapel on that cold February night in 1954, when the "tales" were told and recorded. It is still in use.

while speaking, they were asked to sit comfortably at a table, facing the audience. A tape recorder was placed on the table and, while a few of the speakers seemed a bit nervous over the fact that their voices were being recorded, they soon loosened up and performed like experienced professionals.

The reader will agree, we believe, that the stories that were told that night to the accompaniment of the crackling wood fire in the big pot-bellied stove vividly portrayed life as it was lived during the early days in Grafton. In fact, some writers and historians to whom the stories were shown pronounced some of them genuine classics.

Mr. Pettingill was introduced as Chairman for the evening, and he stated that his stories—for he was, besides, to be the first story-teller of the evening—would follow his introductory remarks. The selection of Mr. Pettingill to conduct the meeting insured the success of the program. Widely known as an excellent speaker and writer, he immediately put the other speakers completely at ease, which caused the relaxed manner in which they all, without exception, told their fascinating stories.

Since no restrictions with regard to subject matter or authenticity were laid upon the speakers, the authors feel it necessary to point out that while some of the "tales" are undoubtedly true, some of them are obviously otherwise. However, in the opinion of the authors, every word recorded that night was genuine folklore.

Since that time in February 1955, all but two of the story-tellers have died. We are indeed grateful that we had the opportunity to record and publish the recollections of our friends and former neighbors while it was possible to do so.

First Story-Teller
THE HONORABLE SAMUEL B. PETTINGILL

The Honorable Samuel B. Pettingill was born in Portland, Oregon, in 1886 and came to Grafton when he was six years old. He lived in the parish house in old Middletown, the first settlement of Grafton, during his early years. He attended the Pettingill School in Grafton, the Burr Academy, and Vermont Academy, and graduated from Middlebury Academy and Yale Law School.

Mr. Pettingill entered law practice at South Bend, Indiana, in 1922 and from 1931 to 1939 was a member of Congress from the Third Indiana Congressional District.

The former Congressman is now retired and lives in Grafton with his wife, the former Helen B. Charles of New York City.

Well known as a speaker and writer on historic subjects, he was the recipient of a Freedom Foundation award in 1960 "for his work in helping to bring about a better understanding and greater appreciation of the American way of life."

Personally, I am very happy about the fact that the stories we are going to tell here tonight are to be recorded, transcribed, and made into a book as a permanent record for the Grafton library. We are all grateful to Mr. Cawley for making that opportunity available to us.

I remember helping Mrs. Francis A. Palmer a bit in

getting up her brother's history of Grafton and I told her I wished it was possible to find enough money to make the history a little longer and to record into it some of the stories of long ago. Not knowing how many copies of the book could be sold and the matter of expense being up in the air, it was kept down to as small a space as possible.

I was talking to Fred Prouty a few weeks ago about how hard our forefathers worked and of the people who settled Vermont. They worked eighty-four hours a week and put in a twelve-hour day. "Men worked from sun to sun; women's work was never done." Just think of the effort those early settlers made in clearing out the virgin timber and in converting the huge quantities of ashes that resulted, into potash, the first money crop made by the people of Grafton. This was true throughout all of Vermont as well. Potash was used in the European textile mills by about 1800.

Of the clearing of forest, the building of the first "ways" or roads, the building the miles of stone fences or walls in the clearing and preparation of the fields for the crops by manpower and the help of oxen, Fred remarked, "I don't think there has been anything like it since the building of the pyramids."

Some day I am going to have someone help me get some facts on how many miles of stone walls there are in the state of Vermont. It would be possible to compute the weight of a yard of the stones and I dare say there was more stone lifted by the people of Vermont than by the slaves who built the great pyramids. So such heavy labor as described before has created a lasting impression—I know I labored under it for a great many years, that everything was grim and stark and hard work for man and wife. For the children as well, who began to help at the age of six or seven years, but it wasn't all labor and heartache. I know that the early

"Stone walls stitch the landscape together. Without their gray green beauty, I think it would fall apart." (*author unknown*)

settlers of Grafton and, in fact, throughout the state, found many an occasion to find moments of happiness. I think one of the pleasures they enjoyed was telling stories about what they had heard from their fathers and their grandfathers.

In addition to story-telling—some of them were tall tales like those told in Texas, but a great many of them were historically important and they well illustrated the lives of the early settlers. Thus history is made.

My great-grandfather, Peter Pettingill, came to Grafton in 1787 with the Reverend William Hall. They brought their household goods in an ox cart, which they drove from Salem,

New Hampshire. The Reverend Hall was Grafton's first minister and he took over the conduct of the church in 1789. He was our pastor for over forty years. So I have the unique experience of being the fourth generation of my family to have lived in Grafton.

To illustrate some of the stories I heard my Father and Uncle John tell when I was a boy, and I wish that I had preserved a great many more of them, there was a family in town named Emery. Noah Emery and his wife had twenty-one children. The story I am about to tell about the Emerys fits in with the cold weather outside tonight. I don't know what the temperature is now, but it was thirty-six below zero at six o'clock this morning.

Grandfather and Grandmother and all the people in Grafton would go to church and, because the church was not heated, they would take with them their little foot warmers filled with hot coals from the fireplace or one of the blocks of soapstone that had been heated in the oven and carried to church in a cloth cover. In time, the temperature of the church would become bearable from those heating devices. Eventually Noah, his wife, and children would arrive. As this procession moved into the church, the door was kept open a long time and the temperature in the building dropped considerably.

Grandfather and Grandmother would feel the cold chills going down their necks and they would huddle up in their shawls. They and the rest of the congregation would mutter, "here comes Noah and twenty-two more."

In 1876, the hundredth anniversary of the signing of the Declaration of Independence, Louis Walker, an attorney in town, gave the address to the people of Grafton in commemoration. He dealt of course with history, largely the background of Grafton. He stated that at that time (1876)

Soapstone objects, the material for which was quarried locally, including bored pipe sections to carry spring water to the houses and a rare foot warmer, from the collection of the late Earl Wright.

there were seven families in town, who had a total of one-hundred and three children. I have heard that up Howeville way there was a school that had an enrollment of ninety-six children, from twelve families.

There was another story which my Father used to enjoy so much and this one was connected with the church. It seems the minister used to conduct Bible classes, and one of the members of his class was a harmless half-wit called Uncle Zeb. I do not recall his last name. It was the regular practice of the minister to talk a while on his favorite topic and he would ask his class for comments about his subject. One Sunday he talked about the Apostle Paul and, when he finished his talk he asked, "Well! Deacon Park, what is your opinion about the kind of person Paul was?" The Deacon said, "In my opinion, he was a very pious man." Well then, asked the minister, "what is your opinion of him, Mr. Culver?" "He was a very zealous man," stated Culver. And so it went, around the class. All the adjectives were used by the various members of the class to express their opinions of the Apostle. Finally the minister asked Uncle Zeb to express an opinion. Uncle Zeb thought and thought, while everyone waited quietly to hear what he had to say. Finally, after quite a long time, Zeb remarked, "Well! in my opinion the Apostle Paul was an Apostle."

There is another story that comes to my mind because of this cold weather. This side of Henry Snyder's house on lower Main Street formerly stood an early grist mill. One of my Father's oldest friends was Wilder L. Burnap, who was born in Grafton and who later became a distinguished lawyer in Burlington. Father and Mr. Burnap served in the same company in the Civil War. His grandfather came to Grafton around 1820. He was a miller who had formerly lived at Ticonderoga, New York. Apparently he had journeyed to Grafton to purchase or erect a grist mill on the Saxton's River. He was a widower and had a baby boy less than a year old. Having concluded his business in Grafton, the grandfather walked the ninety miles back to Ticonderoga in January, and then returned to Grafton, pulling his little son on a hand sled. This is just another example of some of the labor that went into the building of this community, and I think we should be grateful to them for the steadfast endurance and courage they exhibited.

One of Father's favorite stories of the period of 1830 or so was about a man who lived up the Hinkly Brook road, beyond Houghtonville by the old spring place. That was in the days when it was necessary to drive up the hill and down, to get into the village from outlying places, at a much slower pace than it is done today. In those days the local store sold West Indian rum and molasses from barrels. This man liked rum very much and it was his custom to hitch up a horse to the buckboard and drive up the hill and down again to the village every week to get a gallon of rum. He would then drive home again and enjoy drinking his rum until the jug was empty. That drive into town became more and more frequent and he drank more and more rum. To support his drinking habit he had to first mortgage his flock of sheep and he couldn't pay off the mortgage and the sheep were lost. In turn the oxen and, in fact, the farm were eventually mortgaged and lost. He finally lost everything he owned because of his inability to pay off his debts—first the sheep, the cattle, and then the oxen, the farm, and everything else went because this man had driven his horse into town, down the valley, and over the hill to the village too often. Someone summed up the whole experience by saying, "he carried his whole farm over the hill in a jug."

Then there was the story of the husking bee, known and

A Bennington jug of the type that the farmer who lived over the hill from Grafton brought to the village each week to be filled with rum. It was said he "mortgaged his sheep, his cattle, and finally his farm, and lost them all because of his drinking habit," and he "carried all he possessed over the hill in a jug."

enjoyed by our people of an earlier day. Such affairs were the highlight of the harvest season and were thoroughly enjoyed by young and old alike.

At the husking bee, usually held in a barn aglow with light from the lanterns made out of pumpkins and with a plentiful supply of cider and doughnuts. They were gay affairs. This story concerns a Deacon who it appeared was always fortunate in the number of red ears of corn he seemed to find at the husking bees. It was the custom that whichever man found a red ear of corn had the privilege of kissing the woman next to him. The Deacon, it appeared, exacted a kiss from practically every woman present at one bee. He was having a good time, helped perhaps by the amount of cider he drank, and it was rumored he always brought a red ear to every husking bee he attended and he used it over and over again.

As would be expected, there was considerable talk around the village about the conduct of the Deacon at one particular affair. As a result the Parson of the church decided to call upon the Deacon and remonstrate with him about his conduct. In the afternoon on one cold day, the Deacon saw the Parson's old gray mare and rig approaching his house. Anticipating the reason for the Parson's call, he thereupon put some toddy on the fire in readiness for the Parson's arrival. When he ushered the Parson into the house he quickly proffered a hot toddy and remarked, "Parson, it is a mighty cold day outside and you'd better drink this. I wouldn't want it said that you caught your death of a cold coming to visit me." The Parson sat still for a considerable time imbibing the toddy and soon he worked up a healthy glow. That made it difficult to tell the Deacon what he came for. "Parson," remarked the Deacon, "I know what you came to see me about. You are going to remonstrate with me for what happened at the husking bee." He continued, "If a Deacon of the church can't have a little fun once a year in the fall at the husking bees, I am going to resign my Deaconship." Apparently he felt that he had a right to kick up his heels on one day in three-hundred and sixty-five.

The home I grew up in was the second parsonage, opposite the Middletown cemetery. It was a big two-story house and Grandfather acquired it when the church was moved from Middletown, over the hill and up the other side of the valley to the present site of Avery Park's home. Father made up his mind that he was going to move this beautiful timbered house. I had heard my Father say that he believed the house could roll down hill, over and over, and that it would not fall apart, it was so strongly built.

Came the great day of the house moving, and all the neighbors showed up to help. They brought oxen, chains, and logs to be used as rollers, and everyone set to work with a will. To appreciate what a job it was to move that large house over the hill, across the valley, and up over another hill into Grafton, look down the steep incline and over and up the old cemetery road, and you will wonder how it was possible to move such a large building over that terrain with such simple equipment. It has been said that this was a feat never before accomplished in this locality.

With long ropes, hitched to twelve or more teams of oxen, and a plentiful supply of good old apple juice, the job was successfully accomplished. It was a great engineering job even by today's standards.

Following the death of Uncle John who lived in the house in its new location for many years, the place was sold and it burned to the ground in 1912. The sugar house, across the road from the house, became the second school-house in Grafton. That too eventually burned to the ground one winter night.

Down the road near the cemetery was the first pound, and I believe my Grandfather was the first pound keeper. During those days, before the stone fences were built, cattle and other livestock wandered all over the place. It was the job of the pound keeper to collect such animals and impound them until the owners claimed them, after paying a fine of course.

I have often wished that I had written down more stories I knew and have since forgotten, of the old days.

Finally, I would like to tell the story of the old farmer who heard a terrible noise in the attic one night. He grabbed his old musket and crept up the very steep attic stairs. When he could see into the attic, he saw, back in a corner, two gleaming eyes of a varmint of some kind. He took careful aim and let go. Well! the old musket had contained a very healthy charge of powder and it kicked the farmer downstairs and he landed at the bottom with a crash that shook the house. His wife came running from the bed room and asked, "Zebulin, be ye hurted?" Her husband replied, "Woman, climb up the stairs and see if I hit that varmint. If I didn't, I'm hurted bad."

Second Story-Teller:
THE LATE CURTIS TUTTLE

Curtis Tuttle was a long-time and highly respected resident of Grafton. His blooming health and geniality belied the number of years he had lived. Too often the people of this community and, in fact, most other places, take such a rare person-

*ality for granted, but the truth is, such people are living
bridges between the present generations and our past history.
They are, in fact, the makers of our history.*

*Curtis Tuttle was born in a log cabin near Howeville in
1884 and moved to Grafton later on. His wife, Maude, was
born here, and she attended the old Pettingill School.*

*Mr. Tuttle was a Past Master of the local Grange, a mem-
ber of the South Congregational Church, and a member of the
Saxton's River Odd Fellows Lodge.*

Well! the one I am going to tell first is about a fellow
who lived up in the west part of town. He lived on the road
you turn on to get up to the old State Park. His name was
Chicopee Wyman. Chicopee's place was on the right-hand
road above the fork. On his farm the mosquitoes were
awful thick and they used to say that Chicopee raised the
mosquitoes and that he used to tune 'em with his fiddle.

Speaking about the minister as Sam Pettingill did a while
ago, I heard my Father tell about Reverend Hall and Reverend Bradley. Seems in those days they used to have an
hour of church service on Sunday, then an hour of visiting,
and then another hour of service. One Sunday, during the
haying season, a big thunder shower was coming up. I think
it was Mr. Bradley who called the name of one of the
parishioners and said, "I think we should adjourn the service
and help brother so-and-so get in his hay, and then come back
and finish our services." That is just what they did do. They
had to work hard in those days to make a living.

I can tell one about Frank Wilbur's father that is kinda
good. It seems that old Mr. Wilbur used to hire help from
time to time. There was a family that lived in town by the
name of Tusso. Mr. Wilbur, who ran a store, used to sell
flour, kerosene, meat, and meal, the last from which johnny-

cakes were made. One day Mrs. Tusso sent her boy to the store to get a piece of salt pork. Mr. Wilbur sent her a piece of pork commonly called sow belly, with the teats on it. Mrs. Tusso sent the boy back to the store with the pork and told him to tell Mr. Wilbur she had enough tits of her own and didn't have to buy any.

There was another story, about Henry Wooley who lived up above Carver's place. It seems Mr. Wooley had a man working for him who decided one day to quit his job and go down country. I have forgotten the man's name but I will remember it later. The hired man wrote to Mr. Wooley shortly after he left Grafton and said he wanted to join his local church and asked Mr. Wooley for a recommendation. Mr. Wooley had a new man working for him who knew the former employee, so he asked his new man Bill Wiggins "What shall I write down to that church? By hooky I don't know what to tell the minister." In reply Bill Wiggins said, "You write down and tell them he was a good man in a horse race. That is all I know about him."

There is something else I could tell you. This is not a story, but it is interesting I think. Up on the road to the west part of town there was a big stone dam. Some of the stones have been carted away but you can still see what is left of the dam now. The dam was built when my Father was four years old. It was built to provide a head of water to power up-and-down lumber saws.

I'll have to tell one about my Great-Grandfather. He didn't like my Grandmother very much, so one day he told one of his neighbors: "She twan't nothing but a little Frenchman anyway." The neighbor protested, "The other day you said she was an Irishman." Great-Grandfather replied, "That weren't her, that was her sister."

Third Story-Teller:
THE LATE HONORABLE ARTHUR WRIGHT
Former Member Vermont Assembly

Arthur Wright was born on a farm near Grafton and he was well known and respected throughout the area. His devotion to the affairs of Grafton and his many years of service to the community are well known.

Arthur Wright served as a Selectman for a quarter of a century. He was a member, trustee, and treasurer of the Grafton Baptist Church. He was also a member of the local school board, the Town Improvement Association, and the local volunteer fire department.

His genuine sense of humor is evident in the stories that follow.

There is a story you will enjoy about Frank Wilbur's father and Mr. White, when they were in the lumber business together. Seems one winter they were short of help so they put an advertisement in a Boston paper to get some help. Within a few days they hired Mr. Alex Turner and William Early. They were Mr. Grant's father and uncle. These men were put to work cutting timber on the Silas Bruce farm, on a lot I now own. Mr. Early showed me where they had their camp.

A man by the name of Lyman Philips was driving a team

for Mr. Wilbur and, one day when he saw Mr. Turner and Mr. Early, he said, "By golly, you men from the city will freeze up in this country before the winter is over." Well, the men did not say much but before the winter was over Mr. Philips, the native, froze his feet, but the two city men from Boston came through all right.

Speaking of the hard work the old fellows used to do reminds me of a story my Grandfather Wright told me. This was about some fellows who used to cut wood back in the hills. We used to do our chopping in the winter and those two particular men used to like to boast about what they could do. One day the choppers and some neighbors got together and they started bragging about what they could do and one of them said, "The other day I was over in the woods chopping. I always chop one day and pile the next," he continued. "The other day I was chopping and somehow I didn't get around to piling until afternoon the next day. When I got near where I had been chopping the day before, I heard something falling on the trees and, by golly, I looked up and there were the chips falling all around where I had been chopping the day before."

The neighbor said in reply, "Well, you know when I go chopping I usually take three axes with me. I use one until it gets hot and then I take it down and put it in the brook to cool. I keep doing that all day long." He continued, "All day I kept putting the hot axes in the brook and finally I quit working to eat a bite of lunch. While I was eating lunch I heard a noise in the pool where I had put my axes. I went down to investigate and what do you think I saw? There was one of my neighbors scalding pigs in the hot water of the brook."

There was another story, about a traveling salesman who used to come to Grafton from time to time. Residents of the village used to put him up. Had one, one time, who used to lecture about temperance. He stopped for the night at Mr. Culver's. That was the farm where Howard Wright now lives. It was the custom of the farmers in those days to always have a good supply of apple juice during the winter. (Editorial note: Vermont apple juice was of the same potency as "Jersey Lightning.")

During the day of the temperance lecture Mr. Culver did his best to entertain his guest. As they sat around the house, Mr. Culver asked the lecturer if he would like a drink of apple juice. "Well," replied the lecturer, "I don't know as I would. I don't like it very much. I might try one, though." Mr. Culver drew a pitcher of the apple juice and, after a swallow or two, the guest allowed it was good and he and Mr. Culver kept drinking it all afternoon. Before the day was over both men were very contented and happy.

Toward evening Mr. Culver drove his guest down street to the town hall and left him. The next day he was telling some neighbors about the good time they had enjoyed the day before. One said, "Yeah, I heard him last night and I would say he was pretty well qualified to lecture on the evils of temperance."

Fourth Story-Teller:
THE LATE FRANK WILBUR

Frank Wilbur was born in what is now the Will Prouty house, on a lot on lower Main Street in Grafton. He lived most of his life in the town.

For over forty years he served the town of Grafton as a lister. He was the local game warden from 1950 to 1954. He moved to his Townshend Road home in 1948.

During his earlier years he was a cattle buyer, and traveled all over the southern part of Vermont in his dealing and then drove his herds over the mountains to market.

He married Helen Culver in 1911 and was a member of the South Congregational Church of Grafton. He was a Trustee for forty years.

There used to be a man here in town who lived over this side of McWilliams. I used to hear my father tell that John used to buy a barrel of rum, draw out half of it to keep for himself. Then he would fill the barrel with well water and sell it, having cut the strength of the rum fifty percent.

There was something else I was thinking about the other day. It didn't happen in town, but I think you will enjoy hearing about it.

When President Taft was traveling around Vermont one summer, together with his bodyguard, they were passing through Londonderry. At that time there was a toll gate on the road, a few miles this side of Manchester. There was a house on one side of the road and a barn across the way. The two buildings were connected with a breezeway. The toll gate was underneath.

When I used to travel over that road with my cattle on the way to market them, the gatekeeper would lower the gate, which was a long pole, pivoted at one end, and count the cattle. After counting the cattle and after I had paid five cents a head, he would raise the gate to let us through.

When President Taft came by, the gate happened to be up, so he and his party passed right through without paying toll. The gatekeeper telephoned the Sheriff and the officer chased the Presidential party down as far as the Equinox mountain.

At that point of the narration Mr. Pettingill asked Mr. Wilbur, "Isn't it true that Mr. Culver used to repair boots and shoes for the people of Grafton?" Mr. Wilbur replied, "Yes, that is so. I have a book down at the house that Mr. Culver kept as a record of his work." In that book was kept a daily record of the shoe-repair jobs and other sewing that was done. It is surprising the amount of sewing you could get done in those days for fifteen cents or so.

It was the custom of the man who did the work of pegging boots and so forth to stay at the house and be boarded by the family for whom he was working, until all the work was finished. He would then move on to his next customer.

One time, when I was driving the cattle over the mountains, my helper thought we ought to have a little cider. I asked him if there was anyone around who might have some. He told me there was a deaf-and-dumb man down the road who made the best cider around. It seems this man sold his cider for fifty cents a gallon.

Well! We didn't know how to make this man understand that we wanted some cider but, when we drove down by his place the man came out to look at our cattle. I knew we had stopped at the right house as my man had told me it was a place with a big grindstone in front of it, under a shed. The stone was there all right and it was the biggest one I have ever seen, being six or eight feet tall and six or seven inches thick. A shanty was built over it and the stone was run by a small engine.

To get back to the cider, the deaf man came over to our wagon and I reached down and held up a jug. He caught on

One of the many beaver works in and around the village. Their stick and mud dam is shown at the lower left.

and took the jug into the house. It was the finest cider I ever drank.

In about 1890 there were three mills on lower Main Street in Grafton. There was the so-called Gallup mill; the White and Wilbur mill and the Tenny mill. All were run by water power from the Saxton's River. To insure a steady, year-round head of water, each mill had a dammed-up pond or penstock at a higher elevation than the mill. From the penstock the water was fed by gravity through a flume to the water wheel.

The Gallup mill was a sawmill and it was also a cider mill; the White and Wilbur mill was a saw-and-shingle mill. Cider was also produced at that mill and it was sold by the barrel in nearby villages. During the time of high water, in the spring, the mills were run continuously to take advantage of the exceptionally high water. A by-product of the mills was slabs that were sold for firewood. Fred Prouty used to sell them around the village from a little hand cart. I believe that Walter Hemmingway also sold firewood from a cart.

The Tenny mill sawed out chair stock and later made textile bobbins. Succeeding Mr. Tenny in the operation of his mill over the later years were Henry Wooley, Arthur Wait, and Everett Clark.

In 1904 the White and Wilbur mill was sold to A. M. Covey, and it burned to the ground a year later. Covey made cider and cider jelly and he also sawed lumber. The mill was later rebuilt and was owned and operated by Frank Howland, who made stocking darning forms of local hard maple.

I can remember when there were seven schools in session in Grafton—that is, both the village and the township. The village school had four rooms but only two were used. In

1936 the school was burned. The present school was later built on the same site.

Telephones first came to Grafton in 1902. Houghtonville, on Route 121 was a lively place during the early days. In the village there were a number of trading places including a store, blacksmith shop, dance hall, and a Post Office. There was also a sawmill. The village had the usual district school with about twenty pupils. The old stage road from Grafton to Chester was over Route 121 by way of Houghtonville.

The farms in the area were well stocked during those days with both cattle and sheep. One of the largest of these was the farm of Henry Wooley.

This is possibly the largest beaver house in Vermont. It may be seen off Route 121 near Windham Four Corners, in Grafton township.

Most of the one-time prosperous farms have been slowly growing back to alders and brush. In 1955 there were 366 cows, 18 bulls, 200 young cattle, and one pair of oxen in Grafton. In my Grandmother's old account book I found that in 1857 there were thirty-four pair of oxen in the town. At that time if a man had a watch he had to pay a tax on it. They were appraised from five to twenty-five dollars each.

Myra Wooley told me that when she was a girl there were sixty children attending the school in Howeville. Today there is very little activity anywhere in the village. In fact, District One is now practically a forest with few people living in the area.

The Vermont Marble Company and the Stevens Paper Company have planted over 4,300 acres in pine and spruce there and much of it is now being harvested. Curtis Tuttle was born in the old log cabin a mile from the Windham line. It was still standing until a few years ago.

In 1931 a huge fire burned over 200 acres and, before it was extinguished, over 200 men from surrounding towns were called to help fight the blaze.

Our old covered bridge at the foot of Bare Hill still stands, one of the few over the Saxton's River that have survived the floods over the years. Nearby at one time stood a cheese factory, the second floor of which was a dance hall. I don't remember who ran the factory, but I know the dance hall was the scene of many gay affairs.

Many people have asked when the road from Grafton to Townshend was built. I looked it up and find that it was built in 1836.

My Father told me that the first mill to grind grain was on Willie Brook, about three miles up from the main road to Townshend. Some years ago Arthur Wright hauled some of the stones down from the brook. One of those is in the yard of Colonel Adams. It is twelve inches thick and four feet wide.

Round about 1917 I had a herd of cattle pastured up on the town farm. In the middle of the summer several heifers ran wild and disappeared into the woods. They evaded capture until the fall and, whenever one was seen, it was only their tails until they again disappeared into the woods. Well! I heard of some men in Massachusetts who had some dogs trained to trail and catch cattle. I was told those dogs had caught fifty head of cattle that year.

I arranged to have them come up and try to capture my heifers, and within a few days they were on the job. As soon as the dogs were let out they immediately got on the scent and soon we heard them barking. One of the dog's owners said, "By gosh, they have them already." We went over the hill and, sure enough, the dogs were keeping the heifers in a tight circle by running around them. We soon had a rope on each heifer and the men delivered them to my barn.

Fifth Story-Teller:
THE LATE JOHN GRANT

John Grant was born in Buford, South Carolina, in 1885. He left the South at the age of eight years and moved to Danvers, Massachusetts.

He completed a grade-school education and worked at various jobs and finally become a chauffeur in Pittsburgh, Pennsyl-

vania. He worked in that capacity for many years after 1907.
 Mr. Grant married in Boston, and he and his wife moved to Grafton in 1915, where they lived on the Daggett farm, which they owned.

I was married in 1910. I met my wife in Boston and then we went out to Pittsburgh, Pennsylvania, where we lived for about twelve years. I said to my wife one day, "Honey! I would like to buy a place somewhere instead of paying all this rent." "Well!" she asked, "why don't you buy a place in Grafton." I told her I didn't think I could make a living in that one-horse town. She came back at me with, "My Father raised eighteen children there and we lived very well."

I decided to go to Grafton and look for a place I could buy and so got a leave from my job and moved here in 1915. I brought some furniture with me and had it carted up to the old Daggett farm, which I later bought from Henry Wooley.

I didn't know anything about farming but, after Will Prouty moved me to my new place, I decided I would have to get something to do.

In those days they didn't use snow plows. They rolled the snow to a hard surface after every snowfall. Before Will could get my small load of furniture to my new farm, over the narrow road from Grafton, the snow had to be rolled and packed hard. A few days later, when we arrived at Grafton, there was more snow than I had ever seen in my life. Finally the roller, drawn by six teams, got to the place and moved us in.

The first thing the men asked me was, did I have any cider. At that time I didn't know what cider was. Someone said Henry Wooley had some, so one of the men went after it. He soon returned with several gallons. We all sat around for a couple of hours after eating the dinner my wife cooked for us, and then the men drank cider until they got rolling again. I had never tasted cider before but I sure did like that cider.

We had arrived in Grafton on the 15th of March, at a time that seemed like the middle of a hard winter. There was no sign of spring for another month. We lived on the farm until the following December, when we were burned out.

I tried to find work and finally Ed Ober and Alvy Marsh asked me to cut some cord wood for their boss, Henry Wooley. I didn't know anything about cutting wood, but I took the job. I bought a four-pound axe because I thought a heavy axe would cut faster. I was pretty able in those days.

Alvy took me over to the sugar lot, showed me some maples, and left me to my cutting. I cut and worked until I got the hang of it. It took me all forenoon to cut down a tree and all afternoon to cut it up. There happened to be a lot of basswood in the lot and I soon found out it was easier to cut. When my axe sank into one of them, I had to pull hard to get it out again. I finally cut ten cords of basswood. They looked just like maples to me. Alvy came around one day and said, "John, you cut all them basswoods. Mr. Wooley isn't going to like that."

Alvy and I finally drew and stacked all the wood I had cut in Mr. Wooley's yard and we called him out to look at it. Mr. Wooley was blind and I stood back, hoping he wouldn't know I had cut basswood. He felt all over the wood with his fingers and finally said, "A very nice job" and then gave me fifteen dollars. It had taken me six weeks to earn that fifteen dollars.

I am getting away from my story. After I was married

my wife said to me one day, "I would like to take you up to Grafton to meet my Father." I replied, "All right," and so we came here for a few days. We got on the train to Bellows Falls. I carried a little steamer trunk with me. My sister-in-law met us with a pung in Saxton's River. The ladies rode in the pung, pulled by their horse, old Tom, and I walked all the way to Grafton. It was terribly cold and I arrived at the farm two hours before old Tom arrived.

Sixth Story-Teller:
THE HONORABLE FRED PROUTY

Fred Prouty was born in Grafton in 1897 and, except for a few years, has spent his entire life there. He attended the local school and graduated from the Chester high school in 1915.

Early in life he became interested in local politics and has served Grafton with distinction in many capacities: town auditor, school director, and selectman, and he represented Grafton in the Vermont Assembly from 1941 to 1943.

He was one of the original organizers of the Grafton Light and Power Company and was Secretary for many years.

Mr. Prouty is a member and trustee of the South Congregational Church and served for many years as the organist.

In addition to running his own construction business he found time to serve as a trustee of public funds and trustee of the Grafton library, as director of the Ellsworth Clinic of Chester and as chairman for the Grafton Bicentennial in 1954.

He has been more familiarly known to people for miles around for his distinctive service as Grafton Town Moderator.

I haven't any stories of the calibre my predecessors have told but historically I would like to tell one that Frank Wilbur's Grandfather told me about a man named Warren Sherwin. You may remember him. There used to be a camp on the left side of Main Street, before you get to Theron Fisher's. There was a nice house there known as the Sherwin place. Across the road was a house owned by a family named Witherell but before that, apparently, a family named Woolson owned the place, long before my time. If you know your town report you will remember there was formerly a trust fund left by Woolson in the sum of $2,044.44, which gave us a return of sixty dollars a year. This fund was left by Woolson in memory of his boyhood days, spent in Grafton.

Later, after leaving Grafton, Woolson was one of the men who organized several of the internationally famous machine tool companies in Springfield. One of the plants was the Jones and Lamson Company.

Woolson was born in Grafton and he and his family were very poor. In fact Mr. Sherwin told me one time that when they left Grafton, and walked down the road, they carried all their possessions in a handkerchief.

Later in life when Woolson became more prosperous and left the fund to the town and to the Congregational Church, he also left some investment advice. Unfortunately, the investment advice was not sound. The investments and the fund just petered out.

I found this card among the papers of Mrs. Charles Daniels, having settled her estate some years ago. On the card is a notation to the effect that the Barrett house, where the McFaddens now live, "was built in 1787. The Town Hall, across the street from the Barrett house, was built in 1800. The latter, a fine brick building, cost four hundred and fifty dollars and was built by my husband's Grandfather."

At this point in Mr. Prouty's narration, Mr. Pettingill asked him if he knew that the Congregational Church was built for $6,000, and he asked Mr. Prouty if he knew where the bricks, of which the church is constructed, were made. Mr. Prouty said he did not know where the bricks used in the church were made but, since most of the brick used in local buildings were made nearby, it was likely those in the church were also made here in Grafton or nearby. Mr. Prouty also stated that there were two fine houses in Howeville built of bricks that were made right there near the site of the houses. It was the custom in those days to locate a source of clay and make brick by the old method of molding the bricks in wooden molds and then laying them on the ground in the sun to dry and harden. Then they were baked for use in kilns fired by cordwood.

Mr. Tuttle then wanted the floor and stated that there had been a brickyard on the present-day MacWilliam farm.

During my early days, continued Mr. Prouty, there was a beautiful brick house that was known as the Town Farm and which was situated on Kidde Hill. The road to Kidde Hill went through the covered bridge and up Bare Hill.

Here is another interesting fact of our history. Years ago a family named Taylor lived up there. Several of the Taylor boys served in the Civil War. One of them, named Myron, and another called Henry C. Taylor, were the two who enlisted in the Union Army. Their sister was Helen Hamilton, who lived where Earl Wright now lives. She had married and moved to Missouri, where her husband was a teacher of Spencerian penmanship. I have some of his work and it is beautiful. He was struck by lightning while in bed and was killed. Following the death of Mr. Hamilton, his wife returned to Grafton and later moved to Keene, New

Hampshire, where she eventually died at a very old age. However, the thing I wanted to tell you was that Henry is listed as one of the men who died during the Civil War. He died of starvation in the Andersonville prison. Myron, his brother, was also imprisoned there and, when he was given a chance for exchange, Myron got up by the gate and tried to get his brother up there also. The brother was so weak, however, he could not make it and he was left to die.

Myron came back to Grafton after the War and married a girl named Bailey. He was given a job as Sergeant-at-Arms in the House of Representatives. He accumulated some money and they visited Grafton frequently to see Helen Hamilton. I believe that eventually Myron's wife died in the Home at Brattleboro. She left the Home a considerable estate.

On the lighter side, I thought that Mr. Pettingill was going to tell one of my stories. It has to do with rum. Some of us remember another store building on Main Street, between Kabus's and the house where Norm Lake now lives. Grafton, during an earlier day, was a large town. We had nearly two thousand people here and a good many industries. I tore down the store I mentioned. It was larger than Kabus's and was known as the Wyman store. They sold drugs and liquor. It was reported that there was a man in town who liked his toddy but didn't like people to know about it. In those days stores were local clubhouses, with rows of chairs around the walls. The men used to gather in them to play checkers in the evenings. They also pitched pennies, told stories, and even, at times, swapped horses for maple syrup. One day the man of whom I speak came into the store and laid his can down on the counter, as was his custom. Mr. Wyman, the storekeeper, was somewhat of a devil and, instead of filling the rum can as he usually did, without comment, he hollered out, "Mr. So-and-so, you want your usual brand of rum?" That episode furnished food for conversation for many an evening thereafter.

Many of you remember Freeman Cook. He lived on what was called the Baird farm, up Howeville way. I recently bought an old map that shows all the old roads around Grafton and even the farms and house are indicated on it. Freeman was a bachelor. His name was linked for a time with that of an old maid from the village who was very prim and pious. Freeman had been out picking apples for Charlie Davis one day. In those days they used an ox cart with a long platform on which they carried the barrels of apples. The carts had a long tongue extending out ahead of the vehicle. On that particular day Freeman asked the above-mentioned lady to go along and help pick apples. She rode on the cart, standing and leaning against one of the half-filled barrels.

At one point the oxen shied and the cart uptilted violently. Mary pitched up and head down into the barrel with her legs sticking out. She shouted, "Freeman Cook, don't you dare look this way."

A family named Watrous lived one time in what is now the Dorothy Lauser house on the Chester Road. On the back of the house there are unusually large windows and the front door is of great width.

There was a daughter aged eighteen who was so enormous that one of the big circus companies tried to get her to join them as the fat lady. Her parents would not allow her to go and she died soon after. Her casket was so large that they could not get it through the front door, even though the door was a very large one. They had to remove one of the large rear windows and carry her out that way. She is buried in the far corner of the local cemetery and, even today, in the sunken grave, it is possible to see how large she must have been.

There was at one time a set of hay scales in front of Don Lawrence's place. They were later moved up by the Wriston farm. One day Mr. Watrous and some of the boys were by the store, making wagers with each other. They did the most outlandish things. For example, Watrous ate a dozen eggs, shells and all. Well! On another day they were at it again, and Watrous offered to bet he could eat a strip of tripe, six inches wide and as long as the distance over to the hay scales. They wouldn't bet with him because they were afraid it would kill him.

Bibliography

Bellows Falls-Springfield *Times-Reporter,* March 9, 1967.

Fisher, Dorothy Canfield. *Vermont Tradition.* Boston: Little, Brown and Company, 1953.

Palmer, Francis A., and Palmer, Abbie. *History of Grafton, Vermont.* Brattleboro, Vt.: The Shaw Press, 1954.

The Story of Old Vermont in Pictures. Privately printed for the National Life Insurance Company, Montpelier, Vt. Burlington, Vt.: George Little Press, Inc., 1950.

Vermont Life Magazine. Fall 1968.

Wilbur, Frank A. *A Short History of Grafton and Old Reminiscences.* (Private diary, 19?–1955.)

Index

Adams, Colonel, 107
Andersonville Prison, 113

Baird Farm, 114
Bare Hill, 22, 37, 38, 106, 112
Barrett House, 32, 111
Bellows Falls Gazette, 58
Bellows Falls-Springfield *Times Reporter,* 13, 40
Bicentennial 1954, 30, 110
Blacksmith Shop, 69
Bradley, the Rev., 96
Bragg, Mrs. Norris, 43
Burnap, Wilder, 90
Burr Academy, 85
Butterfield, John, 75

Cemetery, Middletown, 94
Charles, Miss Helen B., 85
Cheese factory, 73
Chester Road, 75
Christmas party, 64
Churches: Grafton Baptist, 34, 37,
58, 59, 98; South Congregational,
33, 37, 58, 81, 97, 101, 110, 111, 112
Coolidge Mountain, 20
Coolidge State Park, 20
Crawford, Harold, 43
Culver, Helen, 101
Currier & Ives, 23, 24

Daniels, Mrs. Charles, 111
Darling State Forest, 21
Davis, Charles, 114
Doll House, 75

Early, William, 98, 99

Fellowship Club, Men's, 81, 82
Fisher, Dorothy Canfield, 13, 52, 53
Fisher, Theron, 111
Fiske, Mrs. Rodney, 68
Freedom Foundation, 85

Glenwood Stove, 65, 66

117

Goodwin, John, 40
Grafton Band, 56, 59, 60, 61
Grafton Fire Dept., 63, 64
Grafton Grange, 43
Grafton Light & Power Co., 110
Grant, John, 82, 107

Hall, Mathew D., 68
Hall, the Rev. William, 87, 96
Hamilton, Miss Helen, 113
Hazeltine, Mrs. Robert, 42, 43
Hemmingway, Walter, 104
Hinkley Brook, 91
Houghtonville, 77, 91, 105
Howeville, 90, 96, 106, 114

Jones & Lamson Co., 111
Jug, Bennington, 92

Kenyon, Mrs. Walter, 43
Kidde Hill, 112

Lake, Henry, 74, 113
Lake, Norman, 113
Lausser, Miss Dorothy, 75, 114
Lawrence, Don, 115
Library, Grafton Public, 75, 85, 110
Little, Brown and Company, 13, 52
Lodge, Odd Fellows, 96
Longview, 24

McFadden, Benjamin, 111
McGraw Hill, 17
McWilliams, Edgar, 101
McWilliams, Edgar, Jr., 64
Main Street, 32, 33, 56, 69, 72, 74,
    75, 77, 100, 104, 111

Marble Company, Vermont, 106
Marsh, Alvah, 109
Mathey, Dean, 68
Memorial Day, 53, 55, 56
Middletown, 9, 10, 11, 74, 85
Middletown Academy, 85
Mills: Gallup, 104; Tenny, 104;
    White and Wilbur, 104
Moderator, Town, 41
Mountains: Burke, 21; Equinox, 102;
    Green, 40; White, 18
Museum, Grafton Historical, 61, 76

Ober, Ed, 109
Old Town Road, 74

Palmer, Francis A., 85
Paper Co., Stevens, 106
Park, Deacon, 90
Pettingill, Peter, 87
Pettingill, Samuel B., 82, 84, 96, 102,
    112, 113
Pettingill School, 85
Phelps, Francis, 60
Phelps, Harlan, 78
Philips, Lyman, 98
Post Office, Grafton, 105
Potash Works, 10
Prouty, Fred, 40, 41, 42, 82, 86, 104,
    110, 112
Prouty, Will, 100, 108

Saxton's River, 35, 37, 53, 55, 69, 71,
    91, 106, 110
Sessler, the Rev. J., 59
Sherman, Warren, 111
Snyder, Henry, 90
Soapstone Quarry, 89
Stand Up For America Day, 59, 60
State of Vermont, 62

State Parks, 19

Taft, Pres. William Howard, 101
Tavern, Grafton, 51, 77, 78
Taylor, Henry, 112
Thanksgiving Custom, 64
Town Hall, 32, 111
Town Meeting, 39, 40, 52
Town Moderator, Grafton, 110
Trenton (N.J.) *Evening Times,* 51
Turner, Alex, 98
Tuttle, Curtis, 82, 95, 96, 106, 112

Union Army, 112
U.S. Centennial 1876, 88

Vermont, 18, 19, 31, 38, 45, 51, 53, 67, 80, 86, 101
Vermont Assembly, 40, 58, 110
Vermonters, 49, 52
Vermont Life Magazine, frontispiece, 19, 53, 72
Vermont Recreation & Development Commission, 19
Vermont Tradition, 13, 52
Village Garage, 73
Village Pump, 70, 71
Village Store, 74

Wait, Arthur, 104, 106
Walker, Louis, 88
Wiggins, William, 97
Wilbur, Frank, 82, 96, 97, 98, 99, 100, 102, 111
Windham, 106
Windham Foundation, 32, 67, 68, 71, 79, 80
Windham Four Corners, 105
Wooley, Henry, 97, 104, 105, 108, 109
Wooley, Myra, 106
Wright, Arthur, 98
Wright, Doris, 45, 48, 65, 66
Wright, Earl, 25, 30, 44, 46, 47, 48, 89, 112
Wright, Howard, 100
Wright, Mrs. Arthur, 43, 82, 98
Wriston, John, 79, 80
Wyman, Chicopee, 96